D1614537

BEYOND STILLNESS

First published in 2022 by
The Dedalus Press
13 Moyclare Road
Baldoyle
Dublin D13 K1C2
Ireland

www.dedaluspress.com

ISBN 978-1-915629-03-6 (paperback)
ISBN 978-1-915629-02-9 (hardback)

Dedalus Press titles are available in Ireland
from Argosy Books (www.argosybooks.ie) and in the UK
from Inpress Books (www.inpressbooks.co.uk)

Cover image: Clever Pix / Pixabay

Printed in Ireland by Print Dynamics

The Dedalus Press receives financial assistance from
The Arts Council / An Chomhairle Ealaíon.

BEYOND STILLNESS

MARK ROPER

DEDALUS PRESS

ACKNOWLEDGEMENTS

Thanks are due to the editors of the following, in which some of these poems, or versions of them, first appeared.

MAGAZINES & WEBSITES: *Acumen, Blue Nib, Immagine & Poesia, Present Tense, Raceme, Rialto, Southword, The High Window, The North, The Waxed Lemon, Wild and Wonderful* and *Words for the Wild.* A number also appeared on the following websites: Manchester Metropolitan University's *Write where we are now, Pendemic* and *Poetry India.*

ANTHOLOGIES: *Romance Options: Love Poems for Today,* eds. Leeanne Quinn and Joseph Woods (Dedalus Press, 2022); *Civilisation in Crisis,* eds. Bart White and Dwain Wilder (Foothills Publishing, 2021); *Empty House,* eds. Alice Kinsella and Nessa O'Mahony (Doire Press, 2021); *Local Wonders: Poems of Our Immediate Surrounds,* ed. Pat Boran (Dedalus Press, 2021); *Where The Birds Sing Our Names,* ed. Tony Curtis (Seren Press, 2021).

'Owl' was awarded 2nd Prize in the RSPB/ Rialto Poetry Competition 2018, judged by Michael Longley.

'A Year's Turn' was commissioned for Words Move's Festival in a Van, 2021.

'Coming Down The Mountain' and 'Song of Saxifrage to Stone' were first published in *Comeragh,* Paddy Dwan and Mark Roper, Whimbrel Press, 2018.

'Early Marsh Orchids, Bohadoon', 'River' and 'Otter' played a part in Clonmel's Applefest, 2020, and 'Mountains' in their Solstice: Darkness to Light, 2021.

Special thanks to James Harpur.

Contents

⌒

5

for Jane

Where Does It Hurt

River hidden in the wood,
do you mean us harm or good.

Cicada, without your song,
days are colder, nights long.

Why, Aspen Leaf, do you tremble
when there's no wind at all.

Your flight, Swallow, cannot mend
this torn world it seems to mend.

O mother, put on the kettle,
I am certain of so little.

Bell, you strike the hour of eight.
We all know it's getting late.

Open, Beetle, your lovely back,
try to show us what we lack.

Loving scarf of Atmosphere
we pluck your threads, we interfere.

Grass, prepare your sharpest blade.
They say it's time our debts were paid.

Third planet from the sun,
what have we done, what have we done.

Owl

is that part of a tree
which peels away at dusk
to float out over a field.

Comes under cloak of bark.
Not to be told from a branch.
Finds this to her liking.

Her hunt the stillest of listen.
Open air shaking out
a sudden cloth, her kill.

By day a feathered flask,
where mouse and vole
are silently rendered.

No good the sun knocking
at her door. Only dark knows
how to open her wings.

San Ignacio Lagoon

We can't, it seems, leave each other alone.
Over an hour, she brings her great body to bear
around the small boat. Quick as a lizard dives,
disappears; resurfaces right beside us.
In her own way, playing like a kitten.
Likeness, our reflex: not *like* anything.
Each barnacle, the sea-lice, patches of silver.
An odd, familiar, vestigial bristle.
On her back, at a right angle to the panga,
she displays her pregnant belly. To the sun,
to the sky, to us, she declares with pride,
Behold, I am with child. No doubt about it.
Who knows. Like a huge and heavy dove.
Like again. Still. Just under the water
her eye, a wise and wrinkled fold, appears
to study us, in our element, as our eyes
look down into hers. Steady on. And yet.
A sense that she's smiling. The tip of her mouth
in the air, as if in a smile open. Who can say?
A smile shared between us. That's how we feel.
We feel the length and depth of our loneliness.
She lets me touch her belly – the softness
of her skin, a softness unlike anything.
I am sixty-seven years old, I haven't died
too young. It took four days to reach this place
and I will never leave. Saltwater runs through
my fingers, I understand ever less. I am
sixty-seven years old. Stars run through my hair.

Early Marsh Orchids, Bohadoon

What can they do
but stand in the open
and open their flower?

And would I might learn
before darkness falls
to open thus my heart.

Open House

The house takes place on bog.
When the milk lorry goes by,
our rooms are gently shaken.

⁌

Unseen, unheard, each autumn
thousands of clusterflies
slip into the attic
to sleep away the winter.

A sunny day sees a dozen
seep through the ceiling
to grieve the golden windows.

⁌

A spider's listening device
in every dark corner,
roads known only to ants;

woollens coddling moths,
worms leaving needle marks
in the pages of our books;

dust mites feasting
on cranefly fuselage,
on flakes of our skin.

⁌

The cast of bees
in your studio
after the funeral

which led to finding
the colony of bats
inside the fascia

which led to the bat
entering the bedroom
last thing at night

where it described
in its own good time
circle after circle

Mingaun

A fishing shack
not fifty feet from
the St. Lawrence.

An open window,
glass pinkening
at sunrise.

Lace curtain
lifted and flicked
in seawind.

Rough white wall,
bare floorboard
coming clear.

In the narrow bed
our ears pricked
for a whale's spout.

Rising from silence,
the sudden tree
of sound.

And then another.
A thicket of breath
growing and going

on morning air.
Our own breathing
so quiet – like grass,

like small flowers
in the clearings
between those trees.

Puerto Lopez

I dreamt I was bringing a horse
in from a field.

The long, gentle weight of its face,
the shy watered eye.

The quizzical shudder of breath,
smell of leather,

smell of sweat, ancient grass, faded light,
of meadowliness.

I woke up, went for a pee.
Through a window

I found I could see, in a tangle
of undergrowth,

the round head of a pigeon, fired
by a streetlamp.

Its face was the face of the horse
which was my face.

More Than Ever

Now more than ever, swallow,
is the time to come, up the river
and over the field.

Now, rook, the time to know
your ramshackle basket of twig
holds its fragile trove.

Blackcap, this moment more than ever
we need your hidden delivery,
sudden mad burst of song.

Gorse, your rich and delicate perfume.
Dandelion, your cloth of gold.

Thrush, do not fail us now, sling
your fervent prayer into the wind,
into the driving rain.

Primrose, please, keep sketching your soft circles.
Above a still lake of bluebell,
unfurl, beech tree, your tender leaf.

More than ever, moon, your shining example.
More than ever, pebble, your patience.

March 2020

The Woods

To open the old red teabox
is to free the smoky scent
of souchong, camellia leaf
dried over a pinewood fire.

Cinnamon sticks in their jar,
inner bark of the cinnamon tree
which curls when cut to form
these sweet parchment scrolls.

Orange peel's bitter chemicals.
A pencil's fragrant cedar shavings.
Honey, rich in crab apple nectar.
Willow bark in aspirin.

Darkened with centuries
of wax and oil, consecrated
by the long laying on of hands,
our old furniture holds its own.

And here's the word *book*, from *beech*,
beechwood tablets scored with runes;
or *livre*, from *librum*, once the word
for an oak's inner linings.

We are never out of the woods.

VE Day

I'll never know now what either of them were doing on that day. She might have finished her time as a Land Girl. Air raids were over – he would no longer be needed as a Warden. So perhaps they were together. Neither was the kind for public celebration: let's say they're taking a walk. It's a soft May evening. Perhaps they are noticing and naming flowers; perhaps they have slipped into silence, always their most intimate form of speech. So many things went unmentioned. Next year they'll be married. Why did her mother write to her that way, just before the wedding? *My very, very Precious Girlie … you have only to wait to the weekend to have a chat with Daddy & then all will be well.* She kept the letter all her life: we found it after her death. Perhaps, if it hadn't been written, I might not have come into being. And so might not be sitting at my screen to write this letter, whose last words will be the same. *You seemed so far and I wanted you near.*

Rib Bone

Beachcombed on Achill, brought home,
forgotten until now in altered light
its darkened curve peeps through green,
like a last reminder of a lost race.

Our weight lifted off the earth.
Orchids flower on unmown lawns.
Through the window of our absence
skies and waters clear, creatures slip back.

What if chainsaws in the near field stopped;
if the bog went undrained, if sycamore seedlings
went unpicked and trees grew over the house,
grew over the village, grew over us all?

I scarcely dare admit how I felt,
how deafening the song over my head.

Returnings

1. REGENT HONEYEATERS

for Nancy and Brian

There was the blue of the sea
and the blue of the sky,
unfenced vacancy where eye
could journey, could rest.

There was white scurvygrass flower,
each with seven yellow stamens.
There were celandines, fresh
in a fall of unbroken light.

Marram sang in the wind. Wavebreak
reached out in stray whispers.
A friction of bright gravel,
larksong in the high air.

Let back after so long, I had wanted
to bring to the cliffs only my wonder,
but couldn't forget what I'd read –

those birds, so scattered now, so rare
they are losing their own song,
will soon not find one another again.

2. PERSEPHONE

The track rises through a tunnel of blackthorn,
narrow enough for thorn to catch and tear.

Blossom breaking on black branches.
Dog violet welling through root-cleft.

Is this how she made her way back,
her arms bloodied, her eyes bewildered?

Into an open field at the end of which lay
the enormous surprise of sea.

Lightfooting springy turf to a cliff
where kittiwakes called and called their name

and terns twisted and fell, cutting white flowers,
stitching flight into the bound waters.

3. COMING OUT

On the Mauma Road,
between Coumaraglin Mountain
and a far-off, shining sea,
there we were, birds on the brink
of a nest, unfledged, beaks agape.

Out of house and out of hedge
we were there, larksong running
forward into the future,
soft heads of bog cotton
nodding assent to it all.

The coming of evening over ridge
and valley, dewfall of stars
in the endless dark –
would we ever again
be ready, be able for this?

Somewhere

Somewhere on earth it is
always first light. Somewhere
birds are starting to sing.
The world is washed each day
by hands of light and song –
as if we did no wrong.

Thrush and Blackbird

If, on a raw day in January,
a thrush singing in a bare tree
has the voice of a prophet
wrung by otherworldly zeal,
then a blackbird in May tells,
by the sure rhythm of its hymn,
there is no world to come –
only this one. Calmly praise it.

Nightingale and Cello

From 1924 to 1942 the BBC broadcast the cellist Beatrice Harrison playing a duet with a nightingale.

Late spring evenings she likes
to practise in the garden,
the rich sound of her cello
feeling its way through the dusk.
Deep inside dark leaves
a nightingale appears to respond.

The young BBC wants to try
a live outside broadcast.
She picks Elgar, a family friend –
his halting, heartbroken concerto.

At the last moment, just before
they have to go off air,
the nightingale arrives. Between them
cello and bird do what great art
has been said to do – harmonize
the sadness of the universe.

Sadness, once meaning simply how things are,
bittersweet taste of being here.
Now just *Sorrow*, as if hope
had bled from the word.

To learn ecology, said Aldo Leopold,
is to live alone in a world of wounds.
Nightingales in decline, no longer found
where that cello played.

In the final broadcast the bird, singing alone,
is joined by the drone of bombers.
The duet goes out across the airwaves,
ascends into space. *Help us*, it says –
though there is no help to be had.
Help us, for we cannot help ourselves.

Otter

Your head above water,
wearing a river.

You, river's face,
its appetite,
its muscle.

Your spraint crammed
with its trinkets.

In and out of reeds,
eating the scent
of everything.

Udrá. Water animal.

A name for you
from the start of names.

Nothing so wet.
Coat soaked
even when dry.

Water on your whiskers
always, like love.

River

If I could learn
to dwell in the river –
if I could learn
in the river to have
nothing to do
with myself –
if I could open
a door in the river
and be (as I am)
a flicker of shadow
under the bridge,
a swallow dipping
to sip, weed
in the current,
the gravelly bed –
if I could learn
to go without saying ...

Selfie

Discard
the brittle outer skin.

Undo the translucence
of shell or scale or veil.

At the centre
a thread of green.

Then nothing.

A gate through which
you walk, weeping.

Corpus Christi

They come around the corner
on a cold April morning,
Skin, Suzo, Sticker, Smiley.

Names given to each other,
as if to baptize themselves
into kinder circumstance.

But where the gas sang
and the blood ran from his cheek,
no anemone flowered.

And where her body fetched up
in the river, there was no one
to sing of her beauty.

Skin, Suzo, Sticker, Smiley.
The wind takes their names.

Coum Éaga

It's only in imagination I break the curfew
and make my way on tiptoe
through bog cotton and bog pool to Coum Éaga.

Why Coum Éaga, no one seems to know.
It's dark and cold, facing north.
Cradles no lake. Void of reflection.

Wheatears dash between boulders, flashing
the white arses for which they were named.
Coum Éaga, Death Coum – what's in a name?

Rock is reaching its own slow solution.
Can I pick the trickle of water deep under grass?
Is roseroot in flower, high on the cliff face?

A peregrine starts to voice its alarm.
I mustn't disturb it further.
And I had thought to be so quiet.

Perhaps I'll never see the yellow poppy.
In some dark corner its briefness burns.
I came here when told I hadn't long

to live. The wheatears I saw then are not
the ones I see now. In Death Coum,
what survives? What survives is Spring.

Song of Saxifrage to Sandstone

Let me not be homeless.
Let me gain a hold.

Hide me in your shadow,
root me in your fold.

Let my green leaf wax,
suckled on your seep.

Wear me like a favour.
I will listen while you weep.

Coumtay

Rain opens like a ghost in the valley,
smokes away over the hills.

Funnelled up a narrow gulley
wind roars like a waterfall.

Rain and wind haunt the peat hags,
make red grass blaze, send heather flying.

Rain and wind, quick, vicious crows
pecking the face of Old Man Mountain.

Seven small lakes, Coumtay's gentle heart –
the great stone shoulders which protect it

being worn away grain by grain,
being floored by feathers, wind and rain.

Coming Down The Mountain

You have been
where you have been
someone else,

a place of peat, pool and sky,
stripped by wind
and swept by light.

You have walked yourself
invisible, rock
your bone and motion

and you would like
to walk forever
but you have to go down.

You try to take
something with you:
a sliver of quartz

or a ram's horn,
a special feather,
a piece of eyebright.

They soon fade,
as a pebble picked
from a lake will fade.

What's found up there
lives only up there,
in that high air.

All you can take
is the way, each time,
you're simplified –

the gift of long hours
spent alone
with stream and stone.

Where a raven's call
took all your attention

and news of the world
didn't rate a mention.

Black-throated Diver

The valley contracts
to this black speck
on a black loch.

Loch, valley,
mountain, sky –
the distances
a diver keeps.

He stretches out
and stretches out
a pair of ghost wings.

Only when they touch
unimpeded
the far horizons
can he settle.

He opens his throat.
Around his cry
the miles curl and cling.

Starlings

for Gypsy and Alan

They wait in the wings of their wings,
living scraps of dusk the dusk assembles,
all hiss and twitch in hedgerow and tree.
The valley tensed and expectant,
shadows settling like spectators.
Light fades to just that tone and then
no help for it, the steady files ascend,
starlings each one translated into
one million-winged dreaming.
Until trees breathe the birds back in
your eyes soak up that shoaling glory.
And then those tired eyes come home,
as children do, reluctant, at night,
cold and dark on their skin, like light.

Balloon

The field was full. So slow and soundless
our descent, those eyes and ears
never sensed we hung above.
The hares went about their business,
running, sleeping, feeding, throwing shapes.

Soon our shadow would block out the light
and they would scatter and we would land
with a bump and be thrown from the basket
and laugh and whoop and drink champagne,
a balloon's bright skin flaccid around us.

But not a muscle had moved when we'd spied
the hares. We might have thought we were falling
into a world unwounded by words –
that we could meet those creatures face to face.

Whooper Swans

1. TYBROUGHNEY

When it seems as if it's all too broken
to mend, house flooding, house on fire,
there are these meadows by the river,
in winter a safe haven for wild swans.
'They eat more grass than I would like,'
says the farmer, 'but they need their place.'

All day the swans attend to that grass.
Neat scrolls of turd mark their progress.
Squabbles break out. There are
pecking orders, power struggles.
Lapwing, curlew drift in from the river,
feed close beside. There's room.

A bright field blessed for life is what
I might once have felt able to say.

2. JANUARY

They are too white for winter.
No frost in their feathers, no ice.
And that bright stain of buttercup –
their bills have been dipped in Spring.

3. I KNELT

beside the dead swan in the field.
It was staring up at the sky.
The eyes had been eaten away.

The yellow on its bill was, I saw,
fashioned from small feathers.
I never wanted to be this close.

The wings were open,
earth supporting what once
had needed only air.

The swan lay in the grass,
a patch of newly fallen snow.
Lifted, it was light as snow.

I thought of the Stone Age child,
buried on the wing of a swan –
what ceremony for this bird?

A bride married to everything,
dead in her dress
outside the church door.

4. NOVEMBER

To be there as they reach this station.
To hear again that slow, sad jubilation.

To see the miles let go of each wing,
to feel the breath of wild they bring

to these damp fields. In this green harbour
to watch them furl sail, weigh anchor.

To know this still happens. To know
they will be here tomorrow, and tomorrow.

Once

When I was young, for reasons
unclear now as urgent then,
I spent a night alone in Hadley Wood
on bare ground beside the lake.
I woke to find myself inside
a thick white mist, and for long moments
had no idea who or what I was.

The mist opened. From reeds close by
a great awkwardness broke – a heron.
It rose but seemed to leave itself behind,
struggling to assemble the fragments
of its wings, its long legs trailing.
From its feet water dripped
onto the still water of the lake.

At last it pulled itself together,
rowed steadily away, its harsh *kraark*
as improbable as its appearance
in that once-again whited-over morning.
I must have seen the bird
a thousand times since then,
but I've never seen it again.

Goldfinch

A charm of goldfinch
playing its way
from alder to thistle,
thistle to alder.

Their song sustained
by thistle seed,
soft white seedheads
plucked by white beaks.

Juveniles present,
their faces still plain –
thistle a brush
to colour a cheek.

Round

Seaweed idles in the tide;
around a rock a loop of foam
widens and wavers into
the shape of the butterfly
feeding on angelica flowers
white as the breast of the swallow
whose back is blue but seems
as black as the chough
whose feet and beak are red
as the throat of the swallow
which flies as fast as the sea
moves slow and a curlew's cry
over the water is as loud
as the breaking of waves
is soft on sand as warm
and yellow as bedstraw
as samphire as hawkweed
as the beaks of the gulls
which jab at some dark shape
out in the bay and the swallow
skims over the idling weed

Drive

The flowers ran
almost unbroken
the full four hours
of that drive,
a stream of gold
which pooled
and thinned
and flooded.

Such a long winter
it had been and now
in both my eyes
pieces of membrane
come loose,
stars and circles
across my gaze
which I 'would
learn to live with'.

Into those eyes
the dandelions
poured and poured –
how wonderful
their abundance,
how wonderful
the home my sight
could still provide.

That there was,
among that glory,
an odd seed clock,
odd bare head,

I'd long learned
to live with.

That one day
my eyes would fail?
The flowers
only more bright.

Gulf

Through blue sky above a pool
a flash of deeper blue –
the blue breast of a rock thrush –
a drop of water crossing the gulf
between heaven and hell.

The story in Luke's gospel.
Dives the rich man pleading
with Lazarus the beggar
that he may dip the tip of his finger in water,
and cool my tongue,
for I am tormented in this flame.

Father Abraham refusing his request –
Between us and you there is a great gulf fixed:
they which would pass
from hence to you cannot.

You told me how hard you found it
to preach on this text – the gulf
you had to gloss between
damnation and forgiveness.
I remember your hesitation, that moment

you shared it with me. I remember
your shoes, unpolished, human,
forlorn beneath your cassock.
I remember those later, astonished words –
I fell down. I've never done that before.

The Duke of Argyll's Tea Plant

Sent to the treemonger Duke in 1730,
labelled by mistake as a tea plant – it went
from garden to back garden to wasteland.

I'd been searching for orchids
in the sand dunes at Bunmahon
when I came across the scrawny shrub.

I remembered it from Bongville,
a ruined village through which we'd pass
on our way to the sea for a swim.

A village between Seaford and Peacehaven,
blown up in case of German invasion.
Among the broken bricks, the plant flourished.

Strange how the name arrived from nowhere
and only then was the meeting complete,
only then did I lose track of time.

I turned around to tell you what I'd found.
You were long gone. But who was I with
if not you, in the house of that found flower.

Sunlight and windfall and breaking wave.
Our footprints on the eternal beach.
Washed away, always they well up again.

In The Bleak Midwinter

What shall I give him, poor as I am?

I've sung these words for so many years
but each time it gets harder
and now I cannot sing them for tears.

If I were a shepherd, I would bring a lamb.

Is it I first sang them long, long ago
in my father's church, snowlight
silvering the walls, snow on snow on snow?

If I were a wise man, I would do my part.

All the long gone lives, all the dear dead,
does their presence rise to close
my throat, to soak the eyes in my head?

Yet what I can I give him, give my heart.

Does it come down to that last word –
how the heart ungiven weeps,
where once it sang like a bird?

The Hare

As I dragged the dead hare
from the road, a crack of bone.

Those marvellous feet, mishandled.

Its shadow waits on the moon
but the hare is nailed to earth.

Life List

The Unhoused Sparrow
The Spectral Curlew
The Last Lapwing
The Silent Nightingale

The Absent Owl
The Stricken Harrier
The Spent Puffin
The Curtailed Cuckoo

The Wounded Dove
The Halted Auk
The Ashen Grouse
The Diminished Swift

The Ruined Bunting
The Edible Lark
The Invisible Ouzel
The Quietened Corncrake

Autumn Lady's Tresses

for Jane and Mick

Dai Squint you called me
when I lowered my specs
to peer at the paper.

When I pointed out
the tiny orchid
you only said *Where?*

But I'd been searching
as we walked
across the sandy turf.

I'd wanted to find
autumn lady's tresses
for you, it seemed only fair –

the flower, the name –
now she wasn't with us,
no longer there.

Her quiet demeanour.
Her short stature.
Her beautiful grey hair.

Daphne's Scissors

Should I order more snowdrops, even now?
Almost worth it just for the names.
Rev Hailstone. Daphne's Scissors. Cordelia.

I would cosset them with leafmould,
gift of the trees I've planted here.
I'd have little to do but tend them.

Will there be time to see them at their best?
Time enough for them to clump up,
for me to lift and divide and pass on?

Such brave flowers. Flat on the ground
after frost, buried in snow but rising
always, lifting their small white faces.

The garden table empty, on the chairs
the shadows of friends.
Though I can't stay here forever

I want to stay here forever,
my hands in the earth of this earth.

February

Wind tearing through the oaks,
making their great heads spin.

Sky swollen with rain, as if some god
can't stop weeping.

One marsh marigold flower underwater,
like the face of a drowned child.

A thrush hangs at the top of an alder,
pouring its grief into the air.

Across the water an egret floats,
whiter than anything has the right to be.

Beyond Stillness

He leaves you to ask the questions,
his answer to each a gentle *Yes*.

You've heard it all before, in print,
on screen. You stop being you.

Who left that room and who
somehow found his way home?

Whose tongue, tied at the root,
couldn't tell what it had heard?

Pancreas, it had heard. *All flesh*.
Metastasis, it had heard. *Beyond stillness*.

⁓

My flesh, I dreamt, had fallen away.
They gathered my bones in a basket.

And where, said one, *do you think
is old Johnny Consciousness now?*

And Johnny Consciousness said,
No use looking for me –

*aren't I all over,
in flame, in dust, in wind, in sea.*

⁓

Might not be as bad as you think,
he said, heading in for the biopsy.
Might just be a lymphoma.

I stared at the anaesthetist.
Best of the worst, she said.
And so Johnny no longer free.

Visitant

She appeared
in the evening
at the edge of a wood.

Looked at me,
a look that said,
'Darling, are you alright?'

It wasn't a dream.
She was there
of her own accord.

But she had come,
I could tell,
as close as she could

and soon she faded
and the wood faded
and the look

was left hanging
in the lonely sounds
of the ward.

And maybe
we all received
such visits

and wondered
at their comfort,
what it might mean.

Saint Peregrine

Patron saint of those suffering from cancer

Pilgrim, falcon,
I turn to you again.

Drop on my body
in your teardrop stoop,
flense the mesentery.

Filled as I am
not with rejoicing
but rapid, aggressive growth.

Direct the chemical
as you directed the ray,
coordinates inked on my skin.

Cyclophosphamide,
Doxorubicin, Prednisolone,
Rituximab, Vincristine –

if not the touching hand
of the crucified Christ,
this developed regimen.

Lead it down the veins
to the owl-eyed lymphocytes,
let lysis occur.

Confess me, Saint.
Make my body come clean.

Holy Water

Do Not Drink.
Only instruction
on the bottle I'm given.

So go on, make fun,
turn it into a joke.

And the prayers,
the poems, mass cards,
retablo, candles?

I come from a place
where little was voiced.

The song we sang
was a song of silence.

Don't turn on the waterworks,
an early teacher said.

I learned my lesson well.

Dark Red Helleborines

Rising through a grike,
leaves like lashes hung
with beads of blood.

Sharp as a blade
the shadow they strike
this moment on stone.

Lapwings

Lifted and laid down and lifted again –
as if the wind had more volition
than these shy birds, whose broad wings
keep leading their thin bodies astray.

Feathers stained by shadows
of sea and moor and mountain.
Crest a question mark, a quiff.
Cry, the lonely fetch and echo of itself.

Beat of whose wings you listened for
in childhood's endless meadows,
and later knew as an eerie applause
when cold drove them close to home.

Lipwingle, Teuchit, Horny Wick, Wipe –
all the names we found to love them.
Ploughmen would gently lift their eggs
and place them in newly turned earth.

Gloss

The tight swerve
    around the bush,
past my window
    into the shed
and out, the dip
    and dart about
the sky and the veer
    back down
and each time
    the shock
at the swoop
    through my eyes,
then the mistake,
    a curve taken
by one bird
    too fast,
window glass
    taken for space –
a slight struggle
    when lifted,
a beak closing,
    ghost given up
but not the gloss,
    nightblue,
not the secret
    in the black eye
and next morning
    past my window
there are
    two birds again –
such instant repair
    and, too good

to be wasted
    on answers,
such questions

Haunt

A dream stayed with me
the whole of the day –
as if the crown of a tree
found itself frozen
in the shape imparted
by a passing breeze.

I was on my knees
at work in the garden.
There was no need
to look behind.
I knew who was there.

He was undoing my coat.
Underneath I was whole.

Open Air

Red wings on the shed's white door –
a butterfly taking its chances.

A thrush washes his song in morning;
on the roof, a wagtail's ballet.

Heaviness of the self, its stumble
and blunder, its never quite knowing.

Imagine: someone steps out of you
and walks into the day on steady feet.

The air opens to allow him room;
without thinking, he enters into things.

An early moon. Over the farm,
like snowdrops, stars.

Token

I cannot piece together that pace egg,
dyed with primrose flower and onion skin,
which slipped from my mother's special shelf,

any more than you can conjure up
the whereabouts of that mizpah ring,
worn thin by the women of your family.

It's too late now to hope to know
the tsip and tseep of a Bachman's warbler,
or the night-delight of a laughing owl.

And though fashioned from clay collected
in Passchendaele where so many drowned,
this bowl holds nothing but silence.

Who knew how blossom falling from a pear
could bring such blinding sorrow; or how
our hands were made for waving goodbye.

Or how, one dark morning, a spider's web,
joining wing mirror to car door, joins
also, for a moment, heaven and earth.

Mountain Grove

1.

Soft fingers of cloud combing the trees.
The smell of leaf mould and mud's the smell
of mud my penknife cleans from a football boot.

Wind entangled in beech leaf and bramble.
Far-off sound of a thrush in another wood.
My name being called across endless dusks.

Is that a wet sack in the ditch or the jumper
I hid because I spilt ink over it?
Rows of white reindeer on red cotton.

Here's ivy I cut to climb a drainpipe
to get at pigeon eggs. All those blown eggs
in their trays of sawdust, the nuthatch egg

I swallow being chased through woods.
And here's the first nest I ever found,
soft moss in the fork of an apple branch.

In a pool by the bridge the small foot
I cut wide open. On my foot the old scar.
Knock of branches, which could be the knock

of a woodpecker, or of the hammer
my father left me, which I've used
for forty years but cannot call my own.

2.

It always happens like this,
leaves lighting up, letting go,
great trunks coming clear.

I kick my way through drifts
as I used to going to school,
and every gap between trees

is a door through which
what's been lost might return.
Ferns like quiet carvings,

twigs like tracery overhead –
on a still November day
it's only a matter of time

before the dead appear,
although they never do,
a jay screeches, I walk on

through scent of mud
and fallen-leaf-loveliness,
this one incarnation.

3.

Undisturbed, the wood's quiet,
by croon of pigeon or screech of jay.

Rungs of root lead down to a stream
whose busy spillings only deepen it.

A rounded stone is an egg of quiet.
It lives in light on ivy and holly.

Not all there when I leave the wood
I must sit for a while in the car.

Whose face is that in the mirror?
Quiet, how would you have me live?

Lodgers

In the dormitory
the small bell sounds.

Lights out the sign
for them to rise.

Into the playground
of evening they rush,

schoolkids pulling on
their brown blazers,

the darlings of dark,
night's tiny navigators.

At dawn they return
to sip from the pond

and do not disturb us
as they re-enter

a house they know
only by sound.

A Year's Turn

The sun lies wrecked
on Gortrush Wood.

A full moon hoists itself
over Falconer's Hill.

Above a ploughed field
on Silver Springs road

a wing of golden plovers
has risen so high

it can only be seen,
in the blue dark,

when the birds turn,
and their white breasts

are touched
and are touched

by the dying,
by the rising light.

March

Out of the river they melt,
the colour of river.

Low March light
silvers the pair,

almost the only way
we can tell them

from ripple or snag,
so much are they

part of the river.
A buzzard, a thrush,

and then a crying
like that of a child.

The river swollen
with rain, reed-thatch

heaped on the path,
a log jammed in a gate.

Thin white mist
that comes at this time,

sky a soft blue, ready
for its swallows.

The otters still there,
all knot and knead,

sailing downriver,
passed as if

from couple
to couple on the bank.

All of us beaming
like new parents.

A crying like
that of a child.

Snow

i.m. Jean Valentine

Snow falling on the river.
A kingfisher fishing
at the shadowy bank –
blue bud on alder,
blue leaf on an oak tree,
blue ghost in a willow.
And your death a blue boat
in snow – *la chalupa,*
the boat you built once, slowly,
in the yard, after school –
little boat in snow falling
on the river, blue boat
shining as it goes through,
and then, shining.

Lines in italics from Jean Valentine's poem 'The Boat'

Floods

Great panes of water glazing
the fields opposite our home –
how soon we get used to them.

They bring the sky down to earth.
Gulls drift in fallen cloud.
An oak puzzles over its reflection.

On clear nights stars glitter there –
how soon we get used to it,
the ground under our feet, going.

Dragonfly

The red nail
of your body
on the table
beside my arm.

Wet glisten
of wing,
membrane
and delicate vein.

I do not want
to touch. What
I want is you
not to fly away.

If I keep still
and if my shadow
keeps still,
will you stay?

I feel more lonely
than words can say.
Cold-blooded
companion,

may I rest
my mind's pain,
if only
for a moment,

in the red nail
of your body,
wet glisten
of your wing?

Pebble

Speak to me, pebble, about the sea,
tell me how it picks a piece of rock
and cuts, carves, buffs, burnishes
to fashion this one particular oval.

And why, of millions on the beach,
are you the one to catch my eye,
the one that begs to be lifted
and brought home to sit on my desk.

Little orphan of the shoreline,
coin of an unknown currency, I warm
your cold soul on my palm –
I'm hanging on to you for dear life.

And all this leaves you unmoved.
I want to say that in the quartz
striping your red skin I can see
and hear the waves that formed you –

why so bad this need to hold,
how, in your stillness, sea's unstillness.
Well, you might reply, *we both came
from starlight, and before that, who knows.*

Mountains

1.

They're still up there,
my glasses
and my stick –
it's no wonder
I've lost my way.

2.

To be in them again.
Lousewort, tormentil,
butterwort –
the flowers rising
like memories.

To meet old friends,
wind and silence.
Not to find the flower
I came to find.
Not to mind.

Gift

That a hare should appear on your birthday,
feeding in the garden quite close to us,
its ears like long autumn leaves.

That it was listening with its whole being –
to wind and rain a few hours away,
to a field of light stirring on the far estuary.

That it should have heard, long before we did,
the man and his dog coming down the lane.
That it loped off quietly through a gate

but that it then came back, to settle
into its form as evening began to fall,
seeming to sleep but quivering all over

with what its ears were still receiving.
That it should melt at last into shadow
but leave, as a birthday gift, its attention,

so that we sat on in the dark, listening
to warmth leaving the stones in the wall,
hearing acorns falling five fields away.

Usage

Too delicate to open, my father's bible.
The much-dented metal of a thermos.

Prayer flags, colours whitening,
cotton gently weathering away.

Patches of gold our palms have worn
on a bannister's dark brown rail.

The small roofless church in a field:
a grey mare, the vault beside it a foal.

Clean, bright edge of a spade,
the shine where it first enters earth.

In a cathedral, left on a post until
it turns to air, a cardinal's biretta.

Love, your hand in mine, all these years –
the use the world has made of us.

Kilfarrasy

Into pools left by high tide
black-headed gulls arrive,
sweeping red beaks
like scythes over the water.
Sun's last light honeys
the pools they work through.
White feather is reddened.
Wrecked cliff reddened.
So much rock the sea
has swallowed – I stand
in the ghost of its erosion,
I hear the thunder
of a thousand, thousand storms.
No more than a sweep
of one red beak, this life,
and yet my heart is singing.

Mac Duagh's Well

O spring
inside the world,
forgive me
if I haven't
drunk my fill.

NOTES

Page 28: 'Nightingale and Cello'. In a recent programme, the BBC acknowledged that the 'singing' of the nightingale in the first broadcast was in fact the work of a whistler, or siffleur, who imitated the bird with extreme accuracy. In the absence of definite evidence, this has been disputed by Beatrice Harrison's biographer, Patricia Cleveland-Peck.